BLOOD IN THE SNOW

A COLLECTION OF POEMS

BY

JUDITH MATHIESON

Order this book online at www.trafford.com
or email orders@trafford.com

Most Trafford titles are also available at major online book retailers.

Note for Librarians: A cataloguing record for this book is available from Library
and Archives Canada at www.collectionscanada.ca/amicus/index-e.html

Printed in Victoria, BC, Canada.

ISBN: 978-1-4251-9210-5 *(sc)*
        978-1-4251-9212-9 *(e-book)*

Library of Congress Control Number:

*Our mission is to efficiently provide the world's finest, most comprehensive book publishing
service, enabling every author to experience success. To find out how to publish your book, your
way, and have it available worldwide, visit us online at www.trafford.com*

Trafford rev. 08/03/09

www.trafford.com

North America & international
toll-free: 1 888 232 4444 (USA & Canada)
phone: 250 383 6864 ♦ fax: 812 355 4082

Contents

DEDICATION

This book is dedicated with love to:

My family

My friends

My relatives

Wherever in the world they may be

NOTE

Poems with an asterisk (*) are not the same as the original. These poems have been edited.

PART ONE:

MOTHER EARTH… LIFE RUNS THROUGH IT

MOTHER EARTH

Mother Earth, I feel your pain

The humans of my time are destroying you

They give no thought to the consequences of their actions

You once had clean, pure water in your lakes, your rivers, your oceans and your seas

Now most of your water is polluted with nuclear waste and other human-made garbage

The birds that eat the fish die from this poison

When the water is no longer safe for human or animal consumption, what then?

Humans know that water is an absolute necessity for the survival of all species

Do only a few of us care?

I hear the trees crying when they are cut down

The humans from the big lumber companies don't see the damage they are doing

They only see dollar signs in front of their eyes

I realize they have to make a living but when the trees are all gone, what then?

Do only a few of us care?

I grieve for all the animals and the birds and the fish and the flowers that have become extinct

Humans have invaded their territory, their habitat, in the name of progress

Progress?

Does progress really mean the building of more industrial parks, more shopping malls and more condominiums?

Poachers continue to kill wild animals for their ivory or for their organs

Wild, majestic animals are gone forever due to human greed

When the wild animals are all gone, what then?

Will the humans be sorry for what they've done?

Will we miss the howl of the wolf?

Will we miss the roar of the mighty jungle beasts?

Will we miss the thunder of caribou hooves?

Will humans cry in despair?

They might but it might be too late

Wild spaces, wild habitat, is disappearing at an alarming rate

The situation is critical.

Big whaling boats criss-cross the oceans

When the whales and the dolphins are all gone, what then?

Mother Earth, humans have polluted your precious air

Your atmosphere is polluted with chemicals

I can't even pronounce their names

Pollutants in your atmosphere have caused the hole in the Ozone layer to grow larger

Pollution has caused global warming

It has caused drastic changes in the weather patterns

You are rebelling with severe droughts

With floods

With hurricanes

There's no telling what you will do next!

The havoc you dealt New Orleans and other places was tragic

The destruction left behind by the wind and the water was just the beginning

It's a warning from Mother Earth to Humankind.

Human wars have ravaged you, Mother Earth

Rusting tanks and other weapons of destruction mar your beauty

Land mines lie hidden in the ground waiting to injure you

They will injure humans too

Why in the Name of God did we put them there?

Exploding bombs have left gaping holes in your landscape.

Mother Earth, humans of my time haven't respected your precious gifts

Instead they have abused you

They have treated you with disdain

They have misused you

We think we're going to get away with it

We ignore the warnings you give us.

Mother Earth, I hear you moaning in pain

Then I see your revenge

The cruelty

The greed

The stupidity of humankind horrifies you

You follow the laws of God, your Creator

Humans should also follow the laws of God

They don't

Instead they make up their own laws.

Mother Earth, is there any way we can make it up to you?

Has too much damage already been done?

Is it too late?

You remain silent

Suddenly you shudder

Another elephant is slaughtered for his ivory

Another falling tree shakes the ground

Another tornado sweeps through the American mid-west.

Will we ever care about the consequences of our actions?

Will we ever learn from our mistakes?

Mother Earth, is there any hope for humankind at all?

STOP!

Stop!

Please stop cutting down the rainforest

The panda bears and the other wildlife that live there are suffering

We are destroying their habitat for our own needs

Do we not care?

Once the pandas are gone, they are gone forever.

Stop!

Please stop polluting the air

We have to breathe it

The poisons that we spew into the air are making us sick

The number of humans with asthma is increasing

The number of humans with allergies is increasing

The pollutants in the air are slowly killing us

Do we not care?

Stop!

Please stop polluting the water

We have to drink it

The chemicals that farmers spread on their fields

The waste from large factories

This all seeps into the streams, the lakes, the rivers and the oceans

It kills the fish and the water birds

This pollution seeps into the ground water

It eventually kills us

Do we not care?

Stop!

Please stop killing the wild animals

Leave the magnificent tiger

The sleek wolf

The thunderous elephant

Leave these and other animals alone

Stop flooding the land with their blood

Stop using their fur for rugs

Stop using their body parts for trinkets

Even stop using their organs for medicine.

Stop!

Please stop abusing each other

With harsh words

With lies

With loud voices

With fists

Stop killing each other

With guns

With knives

With bombs

With poison gas

Stop scattering body parts across the landscape.

Stop!

Please stop the assault on Mother Earth.

Stop!

Please stop the assault on other human beings whose skin color or culture or religion is different.

Stop!

Please stop!

Stop before the earth and all her wonderful gifts are completely ruined.

Stop!

Please stop!

Stop before there is nothing and nobody left to inhabit this beautiful planet

Stop before it's too late.

Stop!

Please stop!

Stop before we all become extinct.

DAISY

My mother-in-law, Daisy, passed away
A year to the day the towers fell
They were strong
Part of New York's skyline
She was not at all well.

Terrorists destroyed the towers with planes
Thousands of people died that fateful day
There was no warning
No time to say goodbye to family and friends
Pulmonary fibrosis deteriorated her breathing
It took a few months
She died in her sleep early in the morning.

Memories of September 11, 2001
And
Memories of September 11, 2002
They will haunt me forever.

ODIN

When we went to the Toronto Humane Society

My husband, Keith, and I were planning to get a puppy

After talking to us the man said no

We didn't know what to do

He thought for a minute and then he said

"Have I got a dog for you!"

That's how Odin came into our lives

He was a five-year old dog

We had no idea how much he would change us

We had no idea he would act like a god

He's a Golden Retriever

A gorgeous shade of red

I just can't angry with him

When he jumps up on the bed.

When he wakes me in the morning

Whining to go out

I get dressed in silence

Sometimes I want to shout

When he's done his business

He wants to go for a longer walk

There's no way to resist those brown eyes

So again we go around the block.

When I come home from doing errands

He greets me with wagging tail

Keith and I can't leave him alone for long

Or his bark becomes a wail

It seems that we've had him forever

He fits in so well with us

There's no doubt that he's our dog

He's part of our family

He's definitely one of us.

The years passed

Before we knew it

Keith and I had celebrated our sixty-first birthdays

Odin had celebrated his twelfth

Three months elapsed

One morning I woke up and noticed something unusual

Odin had peed on the floor

He never did that

During the day he whimpered a lot

Was he in pain?

He wouldn't eat

He didn't want to go for a walk

Was our Golden Retriever sick?

We took him to the veterinarian

She examined him

The news wasn't good

His kidneys were failing

The choice was ours:

She could give Odin the operation

She could put him to sleep

Keith and I discussed it

We knew this moment would come

We just didn't expect it to come so soon

We did what was right for our big puppy

We didn't want him to suffer.

I believe Odin knew

Before he went to sleep for the last time

He looked at Keith and then at me

He was saying thank you

I know you are my humans

I know you will miss me

I will miss you too

I wish I could stay with you longer

Thank you for understanding

Thank you for letting me go

I know it's difficult for you.

With gentle caresses

With tears

We said goodbye to him

He licked our linked hands

He closed his eyes

A few seconds later Odin was gone

Gone to dog heaven.

NOTHINGNESS

The snow fell on my uncovered head

The cold wind burned my hands

I walked

Then I ran

I didn't care where I was going

It wasn't important

I just had to get away

I had to get away from that place.

The city streets were behind me now

It was almost dark

My legs grew weary

My breath came in gasps

I tripped and fell

I fell into a dark emptiness.

Soon the snow covered me like a blanket

My body seemed to dissolve into nothingness

My mind forget

It forgot the image of that mangled body

That mangled body was all that remained of a friend

It was all that remained of a friend I had loved.

ODE TO AUTHORS

I love books

I don't think that I could live without books

Books surround me

They encircle the room

Which one will I read next?

Which one will I choose?

Murder mysteries

They make my blood run cold

Enchanting love stories

Involving knights of old.

Words of great mystics

They make my soul fly

Words that inspire me

Sometimes they make me cry.

Words on a page

Can take me to another place

They can even take me

Light years away to outer space.

From the depths of their imagination

Storytellers write

Whenever the muse is with them

Be it day or be it night.

Books make good friends

No matter where I am

On the subway

In my apartment

No matter what the weather

A cold rainy day

A beautiful sunny day

Thank you to all the authors

Whose books have come my way.

IT SHOULDN'T MATTER BUT IT DOES

It shouldn't matter if the color of my skin is white or black or red or anything in between

It shouldn't matter if I sleep on the street or in a comfortable bed

It shouldn't matter if I wear a turban or a woolen hat on my hair

It shouldn't matter if I am mentally or physically challenged or never have a care

It shouldn't matter if I'm married or single

It shouldn't matter if I'm always early or always late

It shouldn't matter if I never ride a horse or lace up a pair of skates

It shouldn't matter if I'm a genius or have little education

It shouldn't matter if I'm a carpenter or the president of a nation

It shouldn't matter if I'm fat or slim

It shouldn't matter if I have children or if I'm childless

It shouldn't matter if I live in a country that's cold or one that's hot

It shouldn't matter if I wear hand-me-downs or buy my clothes brand new

It shouldn't matter if I'm a chatterbox or never express my point of view

It shouldn't matter if I live in a house, in a shelter or in a cardboard box on the street

It shouldn't matter if I have a friend or nobody at all to meet

It shouldn't matter if I work at the post office or at the bakery making buns

It shouldn't matter if I'm a newborn baby or if my life is nearly done

It shouldn't matter if I'm a bad person in prison or a child playing in the park

It shouldn't matter if I'm retired from the work force or a new graduate trying to make my mark

These things shouldn't matter at all but they do

Not one of them should matter but they do.

What should matter is that each and every one of us knows who he or she is

Each and every one of us is a human being

Each and every one of us is a unique individual

Each and every one of us is a child of God

Do we treat each other so?

Do we treat each other with respect?

Do we treat each other with dignity?

Do we help each other?

Do we forgive each other?

Do we love each other?

Do we treat each other with friendship?

We are all children of God

It doesn't matter what name we call Him

It doesn't matter about the color of our skin

It doesn't matter about our creed

It doesn't matter about our lifestyle

It doesn't matter about our race

What matters is that each and every one of us knows who he or she is

Each and every one of us is a child of God

Some day each one of us will see God's Face.

RUMOR'S WORDS HURT

I don't remember the color of your hair

I don't remember the clothes you wore

What I remember is the words you said

Words that cut me to the core

The words you said were not true

They were completely false

I don' know how you could tell such lies about me

Your words made me feel like a nobody

Lower than a worm is how they made me feel

Strange thing is I once did the same thing

I know how the woman felt

She felt the same way then as I do now.

I remember the words I said

I used to work with this woman

The words I said about her were not true

She asked me how I could say such a thing

I didn't know how to answer her question

I said I was sorry

She turned away

She felt sad

I felt ashamed.

I want to say something to you

I want to thank you for teaching me something

Something I thought that I had already learned:

Words from a rumor shouldn't be repeated

Words from a rumor hurt

Words from a rumor should stop with you and me.

KEEP IT SIMPLE

Keep it simple.

Three little words that are so very difficult to do

So difficult to do in this world we live in

A world of terror

A world of war

A world of violence

People are confused

They are frustrated

Some are so easily led astray

Not knowing whom to trust

Not knowing whom to believe.

People are anxious

They are over worked

They are stressed out

Some use drugs and alcohol to ease their pain

Unable to cope with life

Some commit suicide and end it all

They will never see another sunrise

They will never see another rainbow.

Pre-teen gangs wander the streets with weapons

Doing violence to other humans

Destroying property

Just for the fun of it

Not knowing whom to trust

Not knowing whom to believe.

Recently two big financial institutions were on the verge of bankruptcy

They had to be bailed out by the government

Now people are worried about their future

Their jobs may be at risk

How could this happen?

Was it greed?

Was it wrong information?

The government spends millions of dollars fighting a war

A war we probably won't win

A war we shouldn't even be involved in

How many families have lost a beloved father or son?

Too many!

How many families have lost a precious mother or daughter?

Too many!

How many more soldiers will return home in body bags?

Too many!

How many innocent people have been killed?

Too many!

Keep it simple.

Is such a thing actually possible in the world we live in?

Is it?

Why is war still raging in the land where Jesus once walked?

When will it end?

Bodies of the wounded and dead soldiers lie on the ground

Blood and guts are everywhere

Another suicide bomber explodes

Killing a dozen people

A dozen more are maimed for life

Why are people so full of anger?

And hate

And greed

They don't know whom to trust

They don't know whom to believe.

Keep it simple.

I will try

What will you do?

Will you try too?

What do you think?

Will humankind really do that some day?

Will we finally get it right?

Will we finally learn to keep it simple?

Is such a thing possible?

I hope so.

I believe so.

Will we learn to live in peace as God intended?

I hope so.

I believe so.

What a beautiful, blessed day that will be!

THE MAN FROM POLAND

Many years ago a baby boy was born in Poland

He was destined for greatness right from the start

He saw many changes during his lifetime

He influenced many minds

He touched millions of hearts with love and kindness

He was ordained a priest

Years later he was elected as Pope

He took the name of Pope John Paul II.

He was a man of prayer

A man of wisdom

A man of courage

A man of humility

A man of patience

A man of faith

A man of action is what he was.

During years of trials and illness

He never once lost his faith in God.

GOD LIVES

Some people say that God has no place in the twenty-first century

Some people even say that God is dead

Some people say that God doesn't even exist

Some people say that God never existed

I know better!

I know that God lives!

God lives in the clouds

In every drop of rain

He lives in every butterfly

He's even in our pain.

God lives in the falling snow

In every beautiful flower

He lives in every shining star

He lives in every minute of every hour.

God lives in the warm sunshine

In every blade of grass

He wants to live within our hearts

All we have to do is ask.

God lives in every loving touch

In every peaceful night

He's in every rainbow we see

He's in every dawn's first light.

God lives in the wind that blows

In every longing sigh

He's in every smile we send

In every newborn baby's cry.

God lives in all of His creation

In every gift we share

He's in every mountain and stream

In every shimmering waterfall

God is everywhere.

God lives in every note of music

In every whispered word of love

He's in every peel of laughter

In every falling teardrop

He's in every voice that sings

God lives in the homeless person on the street

He's in every stranger we meet.

God is above us

God is below us

God is before us

God is behind us

God is all around us

God surrounds us with His Love!

God lives!

EVERY MINUTE

Every single minute of life is precious

Every single minute is a gift from God

The present moment, the now

It is the most precious of all

It comes quietly then slips away

It's gone forever

It will never return

It leaves nothing but memories.

Was it filled with laughter?

Was it wasted worrying about tomorrow?

Did it pass by with love?

Was it filled with sorrow?

Was it filled with anger?

Was it used for saying a prayer?

Someone walked his or her dog

Someone had lunch with a friend

Someone got his or her hair cut

Two lovers made love

Someone snatched an elderly woman's purse

Someone did the laundry

Someone sat in the dentist's chair

Someone gazed at the stars above.

Did a woman give birth to her first child?

What a moment that would be

Did she write a poem?

Did she remember the veterans who served our country in the past?

Did she remember those who serve our country now?

Did she celebrate a special occasion with family and friends?

Did she enjoy the beauty of nature?

Someone, maybe me, asked forgiveness of someone I hurt

Someone else accepted forgiveness

Did anyone listen to a jazz concert?

Did a new mother watch her son take his first step?

Did she listen with wonder as he uttered his first word?

Someone learned a new skill

Someone heard for the very first time the sweet song of a bird.

How will the present moment be used?

Reading a book by a favorite author?

Searching the Internet?

Listening to classical music on the radio?

Paying a debt?

Meeting a lover in the park?

Doing housework?

Cooking a gourmet meal for company?

Comforting a child?

Someone somewhere will be taking inventory

Planning a vacation

Studying ancient civilizations

Writing a short story.

Perhaps the present moment was used to forgive someone

Forgive someone for a wrong long since past

Perhaps it was used to start a new relationship

To perform a daily task

Was the moment used in letting go of a heavy grudge?

Playing solitaire on the computer?

Telling a bedtime story to your niece?

Making homemade fudge?

Maybe you were just being still

Maybe you were giving thanks to the Lord above

Was an important decision made in that moment?

Perhaps to lose a few pounds

Perhaps to break a bad habit

Perhaps to do volunteer work once a week

What a good way to use sixty seconds!

Someone phoned an old friend

Someone played ball with the children

Someone helped a stranger

Someone discovered the adventure that was waiting for him around the bend

Someone faced a challenge head on.

Unfortunately, someone else spent the moment joining a street gang

Terrorizing the neighborhood

Buying a gun

That's not good.

That's not good at all.

How will the moment be spent?

Playing the piano?

No, then how about the guitar?

No, not the guitar

The saxophone

Yes, you've got it

Taking care of someone who's ill?

Gazing at the moon?

Venturing into the unknown?

Taking an afternoon nap?

Writing a letter?

Fighting a war?

Praying for peace?

Will the present moment be spent in the library?

Will it be spent buying new shoes?

Eating an ice cream cone?

Waiting in the doctor's office?

Waiting in line at the bank?

Was it spent in bed trying to get rid of a headache?

Was the moment spent keeping a bedside vigil?

Lighting a candle?

Buying flowers?

Planting a garden?

Taking a tour of whatever city you're in?

Getting a handle on a difficult situation?

Grieving for a loved one who recently died?

The present moment can be spent in watching a new day dawn

On the other hand someone somewhere used it to plant a bomb

The present moment can be used to plant a tree

To hug a spouse

To watch a honeybee busy at work

To observe a butterfly

To watch a rainbow

To help protect wildlife

There are countless ways to use the present moment

Taking the bag of clothes to the Salvation Army Store

Returning the library books

Mailing the birthday card to a friend

Raking the leaves in the backyard

Shoveling snow for a neighbor

Going ice skating

Participating in a street sale.

Surely someone in a place across the sea visited the zoo

Went horseback riding

Wrote an examination

Told a friend I love you.

Did the moment pass by hiking through the woods?

Taking delight in the glory of the autumn colors?

Attending a seminar?

Wishing your parents a Happy Anniversary?

Someone used this moment to build a log cabin

To go to an auction sale

To begin packing for moving day

Someone visited a friend in jail.

Was the moment used to send an urgent plea to God above?

To pray that all wars would someday cease?

Did anyone see the white dove of everlasting peace?

Did someone sit on the beach?

Did a newlywed couple leave on their honeymoon?

Perhaps someone received her first kiss

Rented a room

Swept away her fears with a prayer and a big broom.

Was the moment used for rock climbing?

Hitting a home run?

Playing a round of golf?

Swimming with dolphins?

Jumping for joy that a big project is finally done?

It is possible that someone attended a christening

Took his or her final vows

Found a new job

A woman at long lost found her true love.

What a great shame it would be if anyone used those sixty seconds

To hurt a friend

To spread a rumor

To get behind the wheel drunk

To have an abortion

Someone used them to fight a fire

Someone saved a life

Someone held his newborn daughter

Someone kissed his wife.

Where was the moment spent?

Was it spent on the subway?

Was someone in a traffic jam?

I know that someone was on her way to the airport

I know that someone else was in the operating room.

Was the moment spent at work?

At church

In the hospital

At a funeral

On a park bench wrapped in newspaper

In a shack

In a house

In a courtroom

In prison

Were you in a bar?

Did the moment pass by exploring the mysteries of space?

Did someone cry from a broken heart?

Did someone wake shaking from a nightmare?

Did someone attempt suicide?

Did he or she change their mind and make a brand new start?

Someone had a dream

A dream about peace

About love

About a brand new birth

Someone else had a dream of evil

He planned to destroy the earth.

Was the moment used to arrange flowers in a vase?

Did someone go for an interview?

Pick up the dry cleaning

Prepare a romantic dinner for two

Paint a picture

Graduate from college

Someone I know had a precious vision

A vision of healthy people

Green grass

Pure clear drinking water

Crops growing in abundance

Healthy strong livestock

A world at peace

A world of unceasing love

A world where people treated each other with respect

With dignity

With appreciation

Here, there and everywhere.

How was the moment occupied?

Did you go water-skiing?

Buy a motorcycle?

Go to a dance?

Go deer hunting?

Watch television?

Perform an operation?

Play tennis?

Practice meditation?

Go for a walk?

Was the moment spent at the art gallery?

I pray it wasn't in the deep dark valley of depression

I've been there

Believe me, it's not a nice place to be.

Was the moment restful?

Was it filled with action?

Was it used wisely?

Was it lived with passion?

Eventually every minute ends up this way

From present to past

In the blink of an eye it is gone

It has disappeared into the abyss of time

It will never return

No one can ever get it back

No one can ever recapture it.

Every minute is precious

Every minute is special

No one knows which minute will be his or her last.

Dying is just another dimension of life

Another window

Another door

One day my vital functions will cease

My soul will leave my body

I pray my soul will go to Heaven

Maybe it will go to Purgatory first

To live in God's Light forever.

No matter how I look at it

Life is a gift from God.

BITS AND PIECES

Bits and pieces of broken glass

Bits and pieces of jagged rock

Bits and pieces of cement and steel

Bits of flesh

Drops of blood

Bits and pieces of body parts

This is all that remains of a man.

Why, oh why?

Why, oh why?

Why, oh why must humankind fight?

When, oh when?

When, oh when?

When, oh when are we going to get it right?

Pieces of unfulfilled dreams

Bits of a dying soldier's memory

Thoughts of his grandfather float through his mind

Someone he really wants to see.

Pieces of a falling bomb

Sounds of a child's cry

A woman weeping in agony

As she watches her husband die.

Bits and pieces of war machines
When will it all end?
Bits and pieces of flesh and bone
When will we turn the bend?

Bits and pieces of lives unlived
Someone's son or someone's daughter
Lie beneath the shattered earth
Some are in the muddy water.

When, oh when?
When, oh when?
When will man's inhumanity to his fellow man stop?
When, oh when?
When, oh when?
When will we change a land of hate into a land of love?
When, oh when?
When, oh when?
When will humankind learn to live together in peace?
When, oh when?
When, oh when?
When will all wars cease?

When, oh when?

When, oh when?

When will we ever learn?

Bits of failure, bits of success

Bits of shattered dreams

Pieces of a broken heart

Nothing is the way it seems.

Pieces of day, pieces of night

Bits of wrong, bits of right

A mumbled prayer, a gasping breath

Is this really all that's left?

Bits of green grass

Visions of her face

The fragrance of a flower

A little bit of God's Grace.

Bits of knowledge, pieces of dreams

Is she really holding his hand?

Bits of life flow away

As he leaves this broken land.

He sees bits of a beautiful Light

Is that what they call Heaven's Dew?

He hopes the Light will grow stronger

He hopes that God's peace will shine through.

LOVE'S SONG

Love's song is a warm embrace
Love's song is a smiling face
Love's song is a guiding light
It shines through the darkest night.

Love's song is a faithful friend
Someone always waiting around the bend
Love's song is music sweet
Love's song is the tear we weep.

Love's song is a whispered word
Love's song is a singing bird
Love's song is a flowing stream
Love's song is a waiting dream.

Love's song is a star so bright
Love's song is doing what's right
Love's song is a quiet space
Love's song is a sacred place.

Love's song is sung with courage
The music is different on every page

Love's song is together growing old

Love's song is much more than a band of gold.

Love's song is one of caring

It doesn't matter what the cost

Love's song is sharing our joy and our pain

It doesn't matter what's found or what's lost

Love's song always understands you

Love's song is a song so true.

Love's song grows deep within

The music is sometimes loud, sometimes dim

Love's song is here to stay

Love's song will never fade away.

CHRISTMAS

A new time is coming

A new day is beginning

Will you be ready for Christmas morning?

Christmas is more than store-bought or even handmade gifts
under the Christmas tree

It's more than fine wine, more than turkey

It's more than Christmas pudding

It's more than Mincemeat pie

It's more than love between you and me

It's more than being with friends and family.

Christmas is the Birthday of God's only Son

Some people want to remove Christ from Christmas

There's no way that it can be done!

Christmas is more than a holiday

It's more than just a day of fun.

Christmas is a Holy Day of celebration

It's a day of thanksgiving

It's a day of joy

A day of wonder

A day of awe

Christmas is the day when God gave His only Son to the world

God gave His Son to show humankind a new way of living

Jesus will show us all a new way of living.

This is the time

This is the place

This is the year

Now is the time to know the true meaning of Christmas.

Will I make the time?

Will you?

We say that there is so much shopping to do

So many things to prepare

Is that really a reason not to make time for Jesus?

Am I awake?

Are you?

Are we ready to give birth to Jesus in our hearts?

Is there going to be room at the inn this year?

Are we ready to let the Prince of Peace reign there?

Will this be the year?

SUNDAY MORNING

I walked along the empty sidewalk

The autumn day was bright but cool

The wind blew the falling leaves around

As my footsteps fell softly on the pavement

The leaves scattered before me

To find a place on the ground

I plucked one out of the air

I held it in my hand

On a Sunday morning

FOR MY SISTER

My dear sister

We don't see each other very often

We have such different personalities

Our lives are full of so many different things

We each have our trials and tribulations

We each have our happy times too

For all that you've done

For all that you do

I wish you only the very best

I want you to know

I'm proud to have a sister like you.

JUST WAITING

A teddy bear

Just waiting to be bought

A book

Just waiting to be read

A child

Just waiting to be hugged

A lonely heart

Just waiting to be touched

A Savior

Just waiting to be loved

A Dove

Just waiting

She's waited so long

She's still waiting to cover the earth with a blanket of peace.

SOUNDS...A LIFE SPENT

While walking in the park one summer day

A man heard a loud noise

It sounded like a car backfiring

It wasn't though

It was the sound of gunfire

What a silly person, he thought

He heard the noise a second time

It was much closer

Could it be the sniper?

He had heard something about a sniper on the news that morning

There couldn't be a sniper in this area of the city, could there?

A bullet hit him in the chest

He felt the soft grass beneath him.

He saw flashbacks of his life

Heard sounds in his head

A dog barked

A baby cried

A horse neighed

A woman laughed

A man moaned in pain

Drops of rain hit the window

Wine glasses clicked

The telephone rang

A train whistle blew

Waves lapped against the shore

An audience clapped

A powerful car engine roared

A book dropped onto the floor

Computer keys clicked

Loud voices shouted in anger

An apartment door slammed

Footsteps walked down the stairs

Bagpipes played

Sirens wailed.

The man listened to his own labored breathing

He felt hands on his body

Heard urgent words spoken

Replied "God, I am truly sorry…for all this sins…I have committed."

He felt cold

So very cold

Someone covered him with a blanket

He was still cold

His life force was slowly ebbing away

His blood flowed onto the grass.

He heard a soft voice whisper his name

Felt her tears on his face

She was the love of his life

Was she really here?

He gasped briefly

Tried desperately to get air

He couldn't manage

It was just too much effort

He closed his eyes

Listened for a minute

He thought he heard an angel singing.

IT'S OUR LOVE

It's our love
That keeps us together
It's our love
That makes us one
It's our love
You and me forever
It's our love
It's our love and our special song.

It's your arms that enfold me
They give me shelter from life's storms
What you do to me when you hold me
I've found a place that's safe and warm.

No matter where we go in life
No matter what road we choose
Whether there's happiness
Whether there's strife
With our love
We just can't lose.

The past is gone
Its song is sung

Mistakes were made

Lessons were learned

This moment has just begun

Its bridges haven't yet been burned.

It's our love

That keeps us together

It's our love

Through sunshine

Through rain

Through hail

It's our love

Let's keep it forever

It will still be ours when all else fails.

PART TWO:

CHANGES AND CHOICES

DIFFERENT PEOPLE

How can you know how I feel unless you ask me?

How can you even assume to know my thoughts?

What gives you the right to judge me?

Does it matter if my way of living is different from yours?

We are not all the same

We are not perfect

We all make mistakes

Each one of us looks at life differently.

We are all coming from a different path

Who is to say who's right and who's wrong?

We live each day according to what we believe

Everyone we meet influences us in some way

Every new adventure makes us grow

Sometimes we cry more than we laugh

Sometimes we work so much that there is no time for play

Sometimes we learn the hard way that our priorities were wrong

Sometimes we don't live but we just survive.

There are some things that I don't understand

Why do we destroy our home?

Why do we destroy our world?

Why do we destroy the earth?

Why do we abuse life?

Life is our most precious gift

Sometimes we have storm clouds

Sometimes we have rainbows

Why can we not accept ourselves as we are?

Why can we not accept others as they are?

Each and every one of us is a unique individual

Why do we change just to please someone else?

Why do we not know the value of our own worth?

Every person on this earth is an individual

There is no one else like you in the entire world

There is no one else like me.

COLLECTIONS

What do you collect?

Buttons

Fridge magnets

Stamps

Shot glasses

Teddy bears

Bookmarks

Everyone collects something

I collect words.

OUR ODYSSEY

A few years after we were married

My husband, Keith, and I drove out west

I remember the places we stayed

The towns

The cities

The friendly people

The scenery

The Canadian Rockies

Such splendor!

I remember our trip to England

It was my first time on a plane

I was terrified!

There was no need to be

We arrived safely.

I remember the museums in London

The castles

The mystery of Stonehenge

A country filled with such history

Canterbury Cathedral

This is Wren's architectural marvel.

Then we went by train to Scotland

Scotland!

I loved that country

So filled with history

It's so difficult to take it all in

The clans

The Highlands

The Loch Ness monster

The beautiful music of the bagpipes

The museums

The castles

The beauty of the landscape

Time to leave

Time to board the plane

We'll visit Scotland again some day I thought

And we did.

We're home again

Not for long though

Las Vegas was next on our list

We gambled some

Played the slot machines and won a little money

Went by bus to Hoover Dam

That's really something to see

It's an extraordinary work of engineering

The Grand Canyon and Dinosaur Cave Tour was utterly superb.

I must not forget our trip to Hawaii

The breathtaking scenery

The waterfalls

The Halekea Crater

The Lakani Sugar Cane Train Ride

The Hana Hiway

The USS Arizona Memorial

The Nautilus Submarine Ride

The Sunrise Tour

They are all beautiful memories in my heart

That is where they will remain.

Two years passed

Why don't we go east?

We rented a car

We drove through Ontario and Quebec

We drove the scenic route to New Brunswick

What a beautiful country road!

Historic Peggy's Cove

Beautiful people

We'll visit here again I thought

And we did.

We didn't take any more trips for a while

Years go by

There are family problems to deal with

There is illness

After a long bout with depression

Keith and I take another trip to Scotland

It was the best medicine ever

It was exactly what both of us needed.

The next few years bring more changes

More illness

The move to a new apartment

The adoption of a dog named Odin from the Toronto Humane Society

A death in the family

This last one overwhelmed us

When things settle down

We decide it's time for another trip east

This trip will include Newfoundland

We rent a car and go

Our Golden Retriever comes with us.

We saw rainbows

We drove through fog and heavy rain

Had long days behind the wheel

Finally we arrive in North Sydney, Nova Scotia

It's here that we pick up the ferry for Newfoundland

Port Aux Basques at last!

Cornerbrook to Grand-Falls Windsor

Gander to St. John's

We took a bus tour of that city

Saw cathedrals

Saw lighthouses

Saw little villages

Saw breathtaking scenery.

Time to board the ferry to Nova Scotia again

Stopped at Springhill to see the Mine Museum

What an experience!

Took our sweet time driving back to Ontario

Stopped in Ottawa

Took a bus tour of that famous city

Now, we're home again.

Eight months later we fly to Fort Lauderdale, Florida

Rent a car from Alamo

Next day we board the cruise ship to Nassau

There we take a Glass Bottom Boat Tour

Fascinating!

Later in the day we take a Blue Lagoon Tour

Beautiful tropical fish and plant life

Back to Fort Lauderdale

On to Orlando

Went to the show Arabian Nights

What a wonderful evening!

Two days later we fly back to Toronto

Odin is glad to see us.

We're already planning our next trip

This time we're going to Peru

Peru!

Oh my, what can I say about this country?

It's mysterious

It's beautiful

It's full of history

The Nazca Lines

The Pre-Inca Ruins

Absolutely fascinating!

The Sacred Valley of the Incas

Machu Picchu

Mysterious and exciting

Home at last!

I'm glad to be home this time

I missed Odin!

The following year we take another long trip

This one was to Portugal, Spain, France and Italy

Fatima!

Beautiful, quiet and peaceful

Fatima to Avila

Beautiful rolling countryside

Winding roads

In Avila, we saw cathedrals and statutes

The stained glass windows were magnificent

Now we're in Madrid

Statutes and fountains

Sculptured gardens

Buildings with classical architecture

Spain to France

Narrow, winding mountain roads

Spectacular scenery

Florence is a beautiful city

We saw amazing churches, cathedrals and statutes

Rome!

Rome at last!

The Holy City!

The Holy City with its awe-inspiring marble statutes

Its churches

Its fountains

Its parks

Saint Peter's Square.

Early wake-up call

Early flight

Finally we're home

Keith and I are happy to be home

We're happy to see Odin again

We're very happy to sleep in our own bed.

One more trip was in the works

Here we come, Ireland!

The two weeks went by too fast

They passed by far, far too quickly

We explored your country roads

Winding roads they were

Breathtaking scenery

We had dinner in pubs

Dinner in castles

Saw churches

Saw cathedrals

Saw mountains and rivers

Saw beautiful gardens

We observed sheep, cattle and horses

They were grazing in your green fields

We met friendly people

Wonderful people

Heard stories

Stories about your villains

Your heroes

Your politicians

Your poets

Your writers

We heard Irish music

Saw Irish dancing

Now sadly Emerald Isle

It's time for us to depart

Goodbye, Ireland

Memories of you will remain in my heart.

I BELIEVE

I believe in the sunshine and the rain

I believe in the stars of night

I believe in the birds that sing

I believe in God's Everlasting Light.

I believe in a tender smile

I believe in the sweet fragrance of a flower

I believe in the power of a hug

I believe in the beauty of each hour.

I believe in second chances

I believe in a beautiful song

I believe in quiet places

I believe in righting a wrong.

I believe in a soothing touch

I believe in the rainbow above

I believe in the whispering breeze

I believe in the power of love.

I believe that God is always near

I believe in both laughter and tears

I believe in a beautiful friendship

I believe in the power of prayer.

I believe in music

I believe in the dawn and the dusk of each new day

I believe in flowing waterfalls

I believe in God's wondrous ways.

I believe in Guardian Angels

I believe that all wars will cease

I believe in forgiveness

I believe that some blessed day

Some blessed day the world will be at peace.

THERE WAS GOD

Before the first bird sang his love song

Before he spread his wings to fly

Before the first raindrop fell

There was God.

Before the first blade of grass grew

Before the first tree bore its fruit

Before the first flower blossomed

There was God.

Before the first star shed its light

Before the first wave lapped against the shore

Before the first horse grazed in the pasture

There was God.

Yes, there was God the Father

Creator of all things in Heaven and on Earth

Yes, there was God the Son

He was born as a human baby in a manger

He died on a Cross

He died for the world's salvation

Yes, there was God the Holy Spirit

He gives us strength in times of trouble

Yes, there was God the Father

Yes, there was God the Son

Yes, there was God the Holy Spirit

The Blessed Trinity

Three Persons in One

Before the first lie was spoken

Before greed entered the Garden of Eden

Before the first murder was committed

There was God.

Yes, there was God then

Yes, there is God now

Yes, there will be God for all eternity.

CHALLENGES

Now is the time to be me

Who else on earth can I be?

Now is the time to be set free

From the masks that I wear

From the grudges I bear

If I don't do it now, when will I do it?

I must be the real me

I am tired of trying to be someone I'm not

I must spread my wings and fly

It doesn't matter what the rest of the world thinks

No matter how difficult it is

I must try.

I must live my life as only I can

I must love

I must forgive

Forgive those who have hurt me

I must accept

Accept forgiveness from those I have hurt

I must learn

Learn from the mistakes that I've made

I must live

Live each moment without regret.

Live each moment in the present

What else is there?

Yesterday is gone

What's done is done

What can I do about it?

Tomorrow is far away

There's only today

That's all there is.

I will let my spirit guide me

I will let love lead the way

I see the darkness

I see the light

I see the joys

The sorrows too

I see the pleasure

See the pain

See the loss

See the gain

I will take one step at a time

One step at a time

One step at a time is all that I can do.

I know I must give to life

Only then will I receive something in return

All of my past moments are no more

Their bridges have been burned

The present moment

The present moment is the only thing that's real

The only time

The only time I have to show others how I feel

Sometimes I'm my own best friend

Sometimes I'm my own worst enemy

I'll learn to accept myself as I am

I'll eventually unlock the mystery

The mystery of me.

THE DREAM

Last night I couldn't sleep

I tossed

I turned

I dreamt strange dreams

I dreamt weird dreams

Dreams that seemed so real

Dreams of bloodshed

Dreams of war

Of horses neighing in pain

Of corpses left in the muddy fields

Of disintegrating towers

Of bombs raining from the sky

Of men and women and children dying in agony

Dying in agony on the battlefield

Dying in agony in their homes

Of spirits who roam the world

Of spirits who know that something is terribly wrong

Of spirits who refuse to rest in peace

They refuse to rest in peace until their descendents get it right.

These are spirits of men and women and children

Spirits who know that war is wrong

Killing is wrong

Violence of any kind is wrong

Enough is enough!

Do you hear us?

Enough is enough!

Do you hear us?

We will haunt you day and night

We will haunt you until you get it right

Do you hear us?

Enough is enough!

All weapons of every kind are brought to one place

There they are destroyed

Every one of them

No more guns

No more tanks

No more poison gas

No more killing our brothers and our sisters because they are different

Their religion

Their culture

Their lifestyle

Their skin color

It doesn't really matter, does it?

No more kidnapping

No more torturing prisoners

No more destroying the earth

No more destroying the land

No more polluting the water

No more polluting the air

Do you hear us, people?

Do you hear us?

We are the spirits of past wars

War doesn't really solve anything

Haven't you learned that yet?

Do you hear us?

Will you listen to us, people?

Will you learn from us?

Will you learn from us before it's too late?

Do you hear us, people?

Enough is enough!

From now on it's going to be different

From this moment on

It's going to be different

Do you hear us?

All of humankind is going to live in peace together

There will be no more war of any kind

Humankind is going to live in peace with each other

In harmony with nature

In harmony with all the other species who share this planet with us

The spirits are shouting

Shouting at us

Do you hear us, people?

Do you hear us?

Enough is enough!

Can we do it?

Is it just a dream?

Will we do it?

Will it always remain just a dream?

Enough is enough!

FOR KEITH, MY HUSBAND

God keeps us in His tender care
God blesses the love that we two share

I try to show you every day

How I love you in every way.

Something happened from the start

You did something to my heart

You bring out the best in me

With you I see the world differently.

Even after twenty-five years

My heart beats faster when you are near

No matter how much time slips by

You are still the apple of my eye.

BLESSINGS

I woke up this morning feeling blue

I didn't feel like doing anything

That's exactly what I did

I did nothing

I did nothing except lie in bed

My thoughts were bad

They were depressing

Is this all there is?

Why hand around?

Life is futile

I might as well end it.

I can't believe that I had such a thought

It's true though

I did

A voice said: "Count your blessings."

Was the voice in my head?

Was it on the radio?

It didn't matter

Count my blessings

It sounded like a good idea

I did.

My health I had

My physical health was pretty good

It was my mental health that was upsetting me

I could do something about that, couldn't I?

Yes, I could

My husband was also my best friend

He was my lover

My confidant

We shared a nice one-bedroom apartment

Odin, our Golden Retriever, made three

He filled our lives with joy.

There's more!

I had my eyes

With them I saw my husband's smile

I had my ears

With them I could hear his voice

I had my two arms

With them I could hold him

I had my two legs

With them I could walk with him

I'm not done yet!

All the organs inside my body

All the organs so delicately balanced

They worked together

Each one had its own specific role to perform

That's a blessing, is it not?

Yes!

Yes, indeed it is!

My father and my mother

My sister and my brother

My friends

The few friends that I have

They are good friends

They are true friends

Even my material possessions

My books

My computer

My rare teddy bears

My camera

The pictures on the wall

The television

The CD's

Are these not blessings?

They bring me pleasure

Yes!

They are blessings.

There's one more thing
Last but it's certainly not the least
In fact it's the most important
Jesus loves me
I know now that it was His Voice
It was God's voice that told me to
Count my blessings
I'm so glad that I did!

HANDS

Hands that used to kill

Now caress and soothe and heal

Hands that once were covered in blood

Now build gold castles in the sand

Hands that once held a machine gun

Now hold a crying child.

Oh children of the Holy Land

Is there any way that you can break the cycle of violence?

While the rest of the world prays for peace

You keep on killing each other.

I know I'm not from your land

Maybe I don't completely understand

Why you do the things you do

The thought crossed my mind

Isn't there a better way to solve your differences?

Oh sons and daughters of war

Will you ever join your hands in peace with each other?

TO MY PARENTS

Oh my dear parents
Dad, you are ninety-five

Mother, you are eighty-eight

I feel so very blessed

You are both still alive.

Through all these years you've given me

Love

Wisdom

Guidance

Sometimes we didn't see eye to eye

At times I didn't listen

When I reflect on all you've done

And all that you still do

My eyes begin to glisten with tears

Tears of gratitude

Tears of appreciation

Tears roll down my cheeks.

A heartfelt thank you

Could never express

My deep love for you both

I am very proud mother and father

I am very proud to be your daughter.

THE PATH

The path that I chose seemed so right

It seemed so clear

Why then did I end up in a web of disappointment?

Why did rejection and fear follow me everywhere?

I must have taken a wrong turn somewhere

I sank deeper and deeper into despair

I knew that I had to change my ways

I knew that I had to do it now

I had to do it before it was too late

I needed a friend but no one seemed to care

They had their own problems to deal with

I struggled

I prayed

I struggled some more

I prayed some more

Finally I stood on solid ground again

The first thing I did was to offer a prayer of thanksgiving to God.

I was on a new path

A path that led to love

I was through with taking paths that led to destruction

Along this new path

Along this path that led to love

I met a man

He was heavily bowed down

For years he had been struggling

Struggling both physically and emotionally

He too had been hurt in love

Just like I had been.

We talked for a while

We departed

The next day he phoned

I was delighted!

We began to see each other frequently

As frequently as our spare time would allow

I began to lose my heart

The days passed

The weeks turned into months

I hardly noticed

Neither did he

We were both way up on cloud nine

We were head over heels in love.

Deep down in our hearts

We both knew

We both knew that this was the right choice

We knew that we were each other's soul mates

Neither of us was alone anymore

We had found a home in each other's arms

We were part of each other's lives.

INNOCENT DREAMS

I don't feel like getting up this morning
I just want to lie here and dream
I want to dream
I want to dream the innocent dreams of a child.

Then the thought crossed my mind
Like a river flowing red with blood
Not all children dream innocent dreams.

Some children dream of war
Of violence
Of rape
Others dream of despair
Of cruelty
Of rape
Of abuse
Some dream of hunger
Of thirst
Of living on the street
Of disease

Yes, it's sad
Nevertheless it's true

Not all children dream innocent dreams

Will it be so forever?

If I can make a difference in any way

Let me do it now

Then maybe

Just maybe

One day

One of these children

Will dream innocent dreams

CONNECTIONS

We are connected
You and I

We are connected to the sky

We are all connected to each other

To each other and the universe

To the entire universe we are connected

We are connected to each other

To each other and to every creature on the earth

GINA

A good neighbor
A wonderful friend
That's who she was

A woman with a warm smile

A kind word

For everyone she met

That's who she was

In the last year of her life

She was ill with cancer

She bore it with patience

She never complained

A woman of faith

That's who she was

SOUNDS

I hear footsteps on the stair

A child's laughter fills the air

A dog is barking to get in

I hear the clothes dryer as it spins.

I hear the backfiring of a car

A train whistle blowing from afar

The squealing of a delighted child

I hear the howling of a wolf in the wild.

I hear the whispering of the breeze

The crying of a prisoner brought to his knees

The murmuring of love words during the night

I hear the screaming of a woman running in fright.

I hear the waves lapping against the shore

The ripping of bone as it tore

The roar of a lion leaping at its prey

I hear the questions of a stranger lost in the maze.

I hear the sound of a plane overhead

In the wink of an eye thousands of people were dead

I hear the voices praying for peace

They ask if they will ever tame the beast.

I hear a squirrel scampering up a tree

The buzzing of a busy bee

The pitter-patter of little feet

I listen to the words of Wisdom as she speaks.

I SAY A PRAYER

When I feel weak
When I feel blue
When I feel confused
I say a prayer to You, Lord Jesus.

When I can't sleep
When problems overwhelm me
When my tears drown me
I say a prayer to You, Lord Jesus.

When the shadows frighten me
When fear surrounds me
When darkness is all around me
I say a prayer to You, Lord Jesus.

I say a prayer to You, Lord Jesus
My God and my Savior
My Rock and my strength
I say a prayer to you, Lord Jesus
I say a prayer for guidance
Please lead me to Your Light.

PART THREE:
IT'S NOT TOO LATE

SOMEWHERE THE TRUTH

Somewhere between the earth and the sky
Somewhere between hello and goodbye
Somewhere between a smile and a cry
The truth will set the world free.

Somewhere between the mountain and the sea
Somewhere between the moon and the sun
Somewhere between the hell of war and the heaven of peace
The truth will set us free

Somewhere between the clouds and the rain
Somewhere between the joy and the pain
Somewhere between the work and the play
The truth will set the world free.

Somewhere between this minute and the next
Somewhere between the thought and the action
Somewhere between space and time
The truth will set the world free.

Somewhere between the dark and the light
Somewhere between the wrong and the right
Somewhere between life and death

The truth will set the world free.

Somewhere between fantasy and reality
Somewhere between doubt and faith
Somewhere between ignorance and wisdom
The truth will set the world free.

Somewhere between yesterday and tomorrow
Somewhere between the depths and the heights
Somewhere between forgiveness and reconciliation
The truth will set the world free.

Somewhere between noise and silence
Somewhere between love and hate
Somewhere between the Tribulation and the Second Coming
The truth will set the world free.

Somewhere between the Alpha and the Omega
Somewhere between a stranger and a friend
Somewhere between the storm and the rainbow
The truth will set the world free.

Somewhere between the summer and the winter
Somewhere between the flower and the tree

Somewhere between the sigh and the dream

The truth will set the world free.

Somewhere between slavery and freedom

Somewhere between the west and the east

Somewhere between humans and nature

The truth will set the world free.

Somewhere between the first and the last call for peace

Somehow between nations all wars will cease

Somewhere the world will meet the God of Love face to Face

Some blessed day the truth will set the world free.

WORDS, WORDS, WORDS

Words of acceptance

Words of wonder

Words of love

Words of joy

Words.

Words of hate

Words of frustration

Words of violence

More words.

Words of repentance

Words of forgiveness

Words of madness

Words of praise

Words of gratitude

Words.

That's all they are.

Just words.

Words of healing

Words of jealousy

Words of prayer

Words of death

Words of envy

Words of life

Still more words.

Words of compassion

Words of comfort

Words of hurt

Words of happiness

Words of disappointment

Just words.

Nothing more than words.

Words of sorrow

Words of terror

Words of longing

Words of pain

Words of anger

Words.

Words of encouragement

Words of inspiration

Words of tolerance

Words of humor

Words of wit

Words of wisdom

Still more words.

Words of justice

Words of power

Words of destruction

Words of despair

Just words.

Words between lovers

Words between friends

Words between mothers and sons

Words between fathers and daughters

Words between brothers and sisters

Words between mothers and daughters

Words between husbands and wives

Words between fathers and sons

Words.

Words of the moonbeams

Words of the sunlight

Words of the raindrops

Words of the snowflakes

Words of the bees

Words of the flowers

Words of the birds

Words of the trees

Words of the butterflies

Words of nature

Words.

Words of the earth

Words of the sea

Words of the mountains

Words of the rocks

Words of the sky

Words of the thunder

Words of the lightning

Words of the rainbow

Words somehow lost in the tears of goodbye.

Words of sadness

Words of belief

Words of denial

Words of faith

Words of peace.

What?

Did you say words of peace?

Words of peace

They are so easily spoken

They are just as easily forgotten

They are such important words

I am waiting to hear the words of peace

So is the entire world

Words of peace that will last forever

Words of peace that will never fade away.

Words of trust

Words of justice

Words of truth

Words of falsehood

Words of love

Words of mercy

Words of forgiveness

Words of hope

Words of peace.

What?

What's this?

Did you say words of peace again?

I hope that they are not just words this time.

I pray it is so.

Words of compassion

Words of cooperation

Words of laughter

Words of love

Words of hope

Words of reconciliation

Words of peace.

Words of peace?

Words of peace?

You keep on saying words of peace

Words of peace don't mean anything

They are just words

Not this time!

They said words of peace

Then they took action to make it so

Not an action of war

An action of compromise

An action of cooperation

Listen!

Listen and you can hear it

You can hear the words of peace

Listen to the beautiful sound it makes

Listen to the awesome song it sings

One day it will cover the whole world.

Some day

Some blessed day

The whole world will hear the words of peace

They will be words of true peace

Some day

Some blessed day

The whole world will hear the music of peace

It will be music of true peace

Some day

Some blessed day

The whole world will dance to the music of peace

It will be a dance of true peace

It will be a song of everlasting peace

It will be a dance of everlasting peace.

SIXTY YEARS YOUNG

I've learned numerous things during my sixty years of living

Oops! That should be sixty-one or is it sixty-two

Whatever it is I've still learned too many things to count

I've learned that to compromise is much better than trying to be right all the time

I've learned that to be patient takes a great deal of practice

I've learned that to love and to be loved in return by the right man is worth more than gold

I've learned that after I forgave someone who really hurt me only then was I able to forgive myself

I've learned that the simple pleasures of life are sometimes the best

I've learned that the power of prayer is indestructible

I've learned that owning a dog is not only a joy but also a responsibility

I've learned that the power of prayer is indestructible

I've learned that love is the answer to any question I'll ever have.

Is there more?

Yes!

I've learned that accepting myself as I am with all my faults makes it easier for me to accept others as they are

I've learned that knowing something is wrong and doing it anyway could have very serious consequences

I've learned that letting go of old grudges relieves stress

I've learned that walking is the most natural exercise there is

I've learned that reading a good book is very enjoyable

I've learned that gazing at the night sky fills me with wonder

I've learned that meeting an old friend unexpectedly is always a wonderful joy

I've learned that sleeping in my husband's arms still thrills me even after twenty-five years together

Is there more?

Yes!

There's one more thing

I've learned that love is the answer to any question I'll ever have.

MY UTOPIA

Somewhere there is a beautiful world

I don't know exactly where it's located

In this world there is no war

No violence

No terrorism

No drugs

No street gangs

No unwanted children

There is no global warming

No racism

No discrimination

No manipulation

There is no abuse of women or children

There is no cruelty to animals

People who are physically or mentally challenged are accepted just as they are

They are part of the community in which live they

There are no traffic jams

The only cars allowed on the road are limousines or taxis

People travel by foot

By bicycle

By public transit

Motorcycles are allowed

So are horses

So are dog teams

Homeless people do not exist in this world

There is more than enough affordable housing for everyone

Affordable medical care is available

So is affordable dental care

There is no pollution of any kind

The people in this world do not waste either human or natural resources

Unemployment is non-existent

Everyone who wants to work can do so

All workers have a fair wage

It doesn't matter if they are professionals or factory workers

In this world athletes don't makes millions of dollars per year

The top salary they can earn is six figures

Each and every person is respected for his or her talent

Everyone's gift is welcomed

It doesn't matter how small it is

It doesn't matter how insignificant it seems

Everyone's gift is needed

Everyone's gift is used

There is no jealousy because one person has something that another person wants

If a person wants something he or she works for it

There are beautiful green spaces

There are parks

There are gardens

There are playgrounds for children

Pets too have their own playgrounds

In this world people help each other

They work together to solve any problems that arise

Everyone from the youngest to the oldest is free to state his or her opinion

Unilateral decisions are forbidden

Laughter is shared

So are tears

Challenges are shared

So are triumphs

So are fears

Strikes are illegal

There are no giant corporations to gobble up small family businesses

Companies remain small so that no downsizing or layoffs are necessary

Every working person receives a pay increase once a year

The health care system thrives in this world

Every person has a doctor

Doctors and nurses work in their profession because they want to help people

They receive a five to six figure salary

The people of this world have a say on how high or how low administration fees will be

Every teenager must complete high school

There are no exceptions

It is illegal to drop out

After graduation a student decides if he or she wants to continue their education

If they don't they must enter the work force

Student fees are paid in full by the government of the day

The people elect the government

If any politician – whether municipal, provincial or federal – makes a promise that he or she can't keep he or she can be removed from office

The people have the right to do this

The people are involved in every decision on how their world is run

Every person regardless of age

Regardless of creed

Regardless of culture

Regardless of lifestyle

Every person is treated with respect and dignity

It doesn't matter if a person is living on the fringes of society

It doesn't matter if a person is living in a nursing home

It doesn't matter if a person is in the hospital

All of the people in this world treat each other with dignity and respect

All nursing homes are inspected twice a year

The same applies to day care centers

The same applies to schools

The same applies to apartment buildings

The people in this world use cooperation

They use compromise

They don't use force

There is competition but in a friendly way

Cheating in any way is not permitted

There is no tax on essentials such as food and prescription medications

No one is alone during a crisis

In this world people help each other

They learn from each other

The celebrate life with each other

Death too

They live in harmony and peace with each other

Wildlife is respected

People in this world do not encroach on wildlife habitat

Nature is respected

It is studied

It is appreciated

People in this world live in harmony with Mother Earth

They do not try to control her

Where is this beautiful world?

Does it really exist?

I don't know the location of his beautiful world

I do believe it exists though

Unfortunately

It only exists in my imagination.

CHRISTMAS

It's almost Christmas

What gift would you like to give?

What gift would you like to receive?

What gift would I like?

Nothing anywhere in the world can compare to a gift we already have

All we have to do is accept it

It is the gift that God gave to all of humankind

God gave us the gift of Jesus, His only Son

Jesus, the Prince of Peace

Why is there no peace then?

There was no peace when He was born so long ago

There still is no peace in certain parts of the world

There are still hot spots of war

Hot spots of terrorism

Hot spots of dictatorship

Why can't human beings cooperate with each other?

Why can't we compromise?

Why can't we respect each other?

Why can't we appreciate each other?

Why are we so filled with greed?

Why are we so filled with anger?

Why are we so filled with rage?

Why can't we be filled with love for each other instead?

Why can't we be filled with awe?

Why can't we be filled with wonder?

Why can't we live in peace?

Why can't we live in harmony?

What is wrong with us?

Why?

Why do we continue to destroy not only our own species but also the other species that share this planet with us?

What is wrong with humankind?

Why do we think that we have the right to control everything?

We don't have such a right

How many thousands of year must pass before we get it right?

Why can't we learn from our mistakes?

Will we ever learn?

Another Christmas is almost here

Will we let the Prince of Peace fill our hearts this year?

Will we let the rivers of blood stop flowing?

Will we let the circles of love start growing?

What about the circles of dignity

The circles of respect

The circles of gratitude

Will this be the year?

Will this be the year?

Will we receive the message of love and of joy that the Christ Child gives us?

Will we understand that this is God's only Son?

He willingly left His Father's throne in Heaven above

He was born as a human baby in a cold and dark manger

Will we believe that the Christmas message of peace is here to stay?

Even if we continue to ignore Him God will never go away

God will never give up on humankind.

GOD OF MERCY

God of Mercy

God of Love

God of Healing

God of Goodness

Your only Son left Your throne above

He came to earth

He was born as a human baby

He was one of us in all things except sin

God of Mercy

God of Peace

God of Strength

God of Might

God of Everlasting Light

Help us!

In this modern age humankind continues to crucify Your Son

We lie to each other

We kill each other

We try to control each other

We try to control nature too

We abuse each other

We abuse nature too

We manipulate each other

The earth runs red with innocent blood

It's just the same now as when Jesus walked the earth

The poor

The weak

The homeless

The physically challenged

The mentally challenged

They cry out for help

For the most part other humans pass them by

For the most part other humans ignore them

Rarely do we acknowledge that they even exist

They do exist!

They belong to You!

It's the same now as it was then

God of Love

Help us!

Thousands of years have elapsed since Your Son walked the earth

Humankind does not remember His commandments

If we do remember them we don't obey them

We think that they are outdated

We would rather follow our own commandments

We would rather have no commandments at all

Have we learned absolutely nothing since the world began?

God of Humility

God of Peace

Help us!

God of Love

God of Compassion

God of Wisdom

God of Light

Speak to our minds

Speak to our hearts

Help every individual do his or her part

To help heal the earth

To help heal each other

To help rid the world of war

Help us remove from our lives

The obstacles that keep us from You

Obstacles of greed

Of ignorance

Of competition

Of hatred

Of envy

Help us, God!

Help us to replace these things

Help us to fill our lives with love

With compassion

With cooperation

With wonder

With gratitude

With understanding

Help us!

God of Love

Helps us!

God of forgiveness

Help us!

Then maybe

Just maybe

Future generations will know a world of peace.

HERE, NOW AND FOREVER

Just a few short lines of verse

Dedicated to you, my love

We met somewhere in the great outdoors

In this God's beautiful land

We fell in love

To be

To have

To hold

To give

Here, now and forever

Between the two of us to share

Smiles and tears

Joys and sorrows

And whatever else life throws our way.

We will work hard to make our dreams come true

Our fears we will face together

We will value our time

We will let our love grow

I need you by my side

Here, now and forever.

Until the end of time, my sweet love

I'll hold you in my arms

I'll whisper sweet words in rhyme to you

I never want to hurt you

I only want to care for you

I only want to share with you

My love and my life

I promise to love you

Through good times

Through bad times

Here, now and forever.

PROUD COUPLE

A long, long time ago

I set out upon the road

I was looking for love

I must admit that I had been looking for love for quite a while

It seemed to have passed me by

I thought if it is meant to be

Then it will be

Time went by

Still I waited.

One day something incredible happened:

I met you

I could feel love in the air

It was all around us

Deep down in my heart

I felt the magic happening

Finally I had found the one

The one I'd been searching for

Even then I knew

I knew that our lives would entwine.

Maybe sometime in the future

We'll look back on times and laugh

About how we met each other

We'll know that the wait was worthwhile

You and I together

Down the path of life we'll go

We'll love

We'll laugh

We'll live

We'll learn

We'll cry some too

We'll face challenges

We'll overcome fears

Time will pass

Through everything that happens

Our love will last.

BLOOMING IN JOY

God is great

God is good

He brought us together

He knew when the time was right

We fell in love

We shared our dreams

We conquered our fears

We sank our roots into fertile soil

Stretched our limbs with work

Stretched our minds with knowledge

Reached out for the sunlight of each new dawn

Heard the echo of our song

Felt the warmth of our love as it bloomed

Every passing day it grew stronger.

Twenty-five years have passed

There have been many changes since that day

Since that wonderful day we met

Changes in jobs

In apartments

In hobbies

In health

In lifestyle

In attitude

In friendships

There have been many new choices to consider

Many things have been left behind

Many new things have entered our lives.

There were times of encouragement

Times of frustration

There have been rapids along the way

Times of desperate worry

Times of sorrow too

Our love pulled us through

Our faith in each other helped

Our faith in God gave us the strength we needed

The strength to carry on

There were times of inspiration

Times of confusion

Times of doubt

I recall times of awesome wonder

Times of peaceful rest

Times of joyous celebrations

Times of family reunions

There were times of bad illness

There were bouts of depression

Times of hard work

Of uphill struggles

Of learning

Of adventure

Of yearning

Of trouble

Times when both of us needed an extra helping of patience

Times of winding roads

Of broken dreams

Of sleepless nights

Of goals achieved

Of plans delayed

There was always love to share

Love to comfort us

There still is love

It continues to bloom in joy.

A CHRISTMAS POEM

Candles are burning

Hearts are yearning

For something more

But what is it?

A Holy Child is born tonight

Choirs of angels are singing

Joseph is praying

Mary places the Baby gently in a manger

Angels from on high visit the shepherds

The shepherds believe

They come to see this newborn Child

This Holy Child born for you and me

Born to set us free

Led by a star

A star that shines brighter than bright

A royal star

Wise men travel through the night

They ask in town where a wondrous Child may be found

Nobody can tell them

The star leads them to the stable

They adore the Word made Flesh

They adore the Lamb of God

He was born for you and me

He was born for all of humanity

Born to set us free

The donkey that carried Mary brays

The little lambs nuzzle Baby Jesus

He is asleep in the manger

Love surrounds the earth

At the Holy Child's birth

The cold wind blows

The snowflakes fall

The shepherds return to the fields

Their hearts are filled with wonder

They are awestruck at the sight they have seen

In this day and age

Our minds are still seeking

Our hearts are still searching

For something more

Something more than the materialistic lives we live

God is here

He is always near

He is always knocking at the door of our hearts

All we have to do is to open the door

Just open the door and let Him in

We too can be filled with His Love.

EASTER TIME

Christmas is long gone

The presents are all put away

The decorations are stored for another year

Easter is here!

Easter is a very special time of year

Spring is on the way

New birth is everywhere

Again God shows us

God shows us how much He really cares

The Child born in the stable at Christmas has grown

He is now a Man

He has been arrested

He has been tortured

He has been nailed to a Cross

The Cross that Jesus died on is the Cross of our salvation

On Good Friday Jesus died

How many of His friends stayed?

How many stood by and cried?

Not many

They ran away in fear

How could they possibly do as He'd asked?

They couldn't

Not yet.

For three days Jesus was in the ground

Not many of his friends hung around

Jesus did as He promised

He rose from the grave

His friends once more to try and save

Easter Sunday!

A day of celebration!

A day of triumph over death!

God's own Holy Spirit set His friends free

He can do the same for you and me.

God can set us free from our prison of sin

Show us how to live again

How to love again

All we have to do is to let Him in

Why are we so stubborn?

Why won't we let Him in?

How can we love other human beings

How can we love them if we don't try to understand them?

Do we see the tears in another's eyes?

Do we just walk on after we have criticized them?

I wonder if we would hate a little less

If we changed our thought process

Why don't we help others more when they stumble?

Perhaps we have to be a little more humble

Why don't we let God's Holy Spirit touch us?

The touch would be like the warm wind in spring

If we let Him touch our hearts

If we let Him touch our minds

Then we would praise Him as we sing

Our song of praise would never end.

ONE LAST TIME

I usually take the subway

To my favorite local shopping area

On this particular autumn day I felt like walking

After all it wasn't really that far

The things I saw on that walk

Sparrows, starlings and pigeons in High Park

Squirrels chasing each other up a tree

Across the branches and down again

Beautiful gardens

The flowers alive with color

White

Red

Yellow

Purple

Blue

As I was walking up the hill

I saw an old friend

Someone I hadn't seen in several months

She recognized me as well

We stopped and chatted for a while

We promised to get together for lunch the next day

Then we parted

We never did get together for lunch

That evening she died

She was gone

Dead from a heart attack

I'm so glad that the Lord let me see her

One last time

I SEE YOU

I see you.

Do I really?

Do I really see you?

You are a human being

A stranger to me

You have your pain

You have your joy

You have your dreams

You have your hopes

You are a unique individual

Do I really see you?

You are just another person

You are just someone else taking up space on this earth

In reality

I don't see you at all

All I see is a stranger

Maybe I want to get to know you

Maybe I don't

All I see is another person

Just another person getting in the way of my life.

If I saw you

If I really saw you

If I really saw you as you are

You with all your worry

You with all your loneliness

You with all your frustration

If I looked into your eyes

Instead of looking at the ground

If I looked at your face

Instead of looking straight ahead

Maybe you would make my life better

I'll never know

I'll never know

Until I take the time to see you

To see you as you really are.

A MEDLEY OF THOUGHTS

Sometimes I feel so happy

I'm way up on cloud nine

Sometimes I feel that I can conquer anything

Then one little thing goes wrong

A negative thought creeps into my head

The joy has disappeared

The joy is gone

I'm learning to live with my sorrow

Trying not to worry about what will happen tomorrow

I'm learning to concentrate on today

Tomorrow is too far away

I'm learning to accept things as they come along

I'm getting better

I remember my family members and my friends who have died

Thoughts of them remain in my heart

Thoughts of them wander through my mind

I remember the love they gave me

I remember the things they taught me

I remember them

Every one of them

I love them

I miss them.

I remember the numerous things that have happened to me

The experiences I've had

The people I've met

The pain I've endured

The lessons I've learned

What lessons?

What experiences?

Well, let's see…

To compromise is better than arguing

To forgive the people who have hurt me sets me free

It sets me free from the heavy load of carrying grudges

To accept myself as I am with all my faults makes it much easier for me to accept other people as they are

To frown when things go wrong only makes matters worse

If possible, I try to smile instead

To gaze at the beauty of the night sky fills me with wonder

It fills me with awe

To meet an old friend unexpectedly is a wonderful joy

To ignore personal problems until they become overwhelming is a very bad idea

Simple pleasures are sometimes the best

Simple pleasures like playing with my dog

Reading a good book

Having lunch with my sister

Listening to the radio

Arranging flowers in a vase

Visiting a sick friend

Playing solitaire on the computer

Spending a quiet evening with my husband

There are other things I think about sometimes

Other situations and other circumstances that influence all of humankind

For instance?

Every time a wild animal becomes extinct and is lost to us forever

Every time a river, a lake or an ocean becomes polluted with human garbage

Do you know what happens?

Everyone loses

Every time a man or a woman or a child commits an act of violence

It doesn't matter if it's murder

Rape

Terrorism

Kidnapping

Arson

Bullying

Vandalism

Abuse

Every time a war is started and it drags on and on and on and on

When there is no end in sight

Every time a soldier returns home in a coffin

Every time innocent blood is spilled

Do you know what happens?

We all lose

Everyone of us

Every time weather patterns change due to global warming

Every time a natural disaster occurs

We all lose

Every time one person cheats another

Every time we don't respect a sister or a brother

Every time love takes a back seat to greed

Every time competition is more important than cooperation

Do you know what happens?

We all lose

Every one of us

Sometimes I wander about the mystery of life itself

The universe

Is Earth the only planet that is inhabited?

Is there life on other planets?

I know that every minute that passes is a gift from God

A precious gift indeed

The present moment is the most precious

It comes quietly

Just as quietly it slips away

Then it is gone forever

It's lost in the abyss of time

It can never return

It leaves nothing but memories behind

Memories of old friends

The happy times we shared

Memories of places where I once lived

Jobs I once had

Places I once visited

Things that I did that were wrong

Words I spoke when I should have kept silent

Collections I bought and then sold

Shot glasses

Fridge magnets

Stuffed animals

Books that I gave to the library

Memories of the summers I spent at the cottage with my parents and my brother and my sister

Memories of the day when I met the man who would become my husband

Our first kiss

Our engagement party

Our wedding day

Our first apartment

There are some memories I would rather forget

That's not possible

They are part of me too

Like my bout with depression

Deep in the valley of darkness I was

I stayed there for a long time

Finally

Finally I evolved into the light

Finally

Finally I began to get better

Sometimes I weep at the state of the world

Too many wars

Too much terrorism

Too much violence

Too much pollution of every kind

Too much overfishing in the oceans

Too much poaching of wild animals

Too many trees being cut down

Too many cars on the roads

Too much road rage

Too many people being overworked and underpaid

Too many companies downsizing

Too many companies going out of business

Too many young people committing suicide

Too much pornography

Too much hate

Too much greed

Too much need for power

Too much innocent blood being shed

Too many street gangs

Too many orphans in the world

Too many widows

Too much misunderstanding

Too much corruption

Too much stress

Everywhere!

Where did the Garden of Eden go?

Then I look up

I see a rainbow in the sky

I know that God is near

He is still watching us

He is still helping us

He is still strengthening us

He is still waiting

Waiting so patiently

Waiting for humankind to come to its senses

Still waiting for human beings to learn

When will we learn?

When will we learn to live in peace with each other?

When will we learn to cooperate?

When will we learn to live in peace with nature?

When will we learn to live in peace with the other species that share this planet with us?

When?

When?

When will that happen?

When will that happen?

TEN SECONDS

Where did the bad thoughts come from?

Did they come out of nowhere?

Did they come from the depths of my mind?

Why did the bad thoughts return after all this time?

Months had passed since I'd had thoughts like that

Why did they come back?

I don't know

I only know that they did.

My husband, Keith, and I were involved in an argument earlier that day

He wanted to go out to a political debate

I wanted to stay home

After all, we had been to a political debate the previous evening

I didn't want to go to another one

I'd had a sinus headache all day

It was almost gone but not quite

Our dog, Odin, wasn't feeling well either

I told my husband it was okay to go if he wanted to

I told a lie

It really wasn't

He left.

A few minutes later it happened

The bad thoughts entered my head

The suicidal thoughts flooded my mind

Ten seconds

Maybe twelve

Maybe it doesn't sound like much

Believe me, it was a lifetime

I glanced at the scissors

I glanced at the knife

The knife would do a better job

My hand reached for it

Another thought tried to push the first one away

No!

No!

No!

No!

That's what my mind screamed

What in the name of heaven and earth are you doing?

Do something else

Anything

Anything at all

Hug the dog

Read a book

Phone a friend

Say a prayer

Play solitaire on the computer

Write a poem

Organize your photographs

There are dozens of things you can do

There is no reason for you to pick up that knife

Unless you're going to cut some cheese

If you're going to put it against your wrist

That's something you don't want to do

Do you hear me?

Do you understand me?

It doesn't matter what you do

Just do something else

Anything else

Do you understand?

Don't put that knife against your wrist

Do you hear me?

Don't do it!

Don't do it!

Don't do it!

Don't do it!

You know that once it's done then it's done forever

There are no more chances

Don't you dare do it!

Life is futile, the bad thoughts said

Just do it

Get it over with

No!

Odin would whine and bark until Keith got home

Keith would go mad with worry and fear

So don't do it!

For the love of God don't do it!

I phoned a friend

I got her answering machine

That didn't help

See, the bad thoughts said

Nobody cares about you

Just end it all

You'll feel better

No!

I said a prayer

I had to get out of the apartment

I took Odin for a short walk

The fresh air helped clear my mind of the cobwebs

The bad thoughts disappeared into thin air

I didn't do it!

The good thoughts won

When Odin and I got home I played solitaire the old-fashioned way.

THIS PRECISE MOMENT

This rock

This tree

This snowflake

This sea

Each one is unique

I know it will never be seen in the same way again

As it is in this precise moment

This butterfly

This flower

This raindrop

This hour

Each one is unique

I know it will never be seen in the same way again

As it is in this precise moment.

This sky

This moon

This street

This room

Each one is unique

I know it will never be seen in the same way again

As it is in this precise moment

This laughter

This face

This smile

This place

Each one is unique

I know it will never be seen in the same way again

As it is in this precise moment

This pain

This bird

This leaf

This word

Each one is unique

I know it will never be seen in the same way again

As it is in this precise moment

This moment

This prayer

This sunrise

This chair

Each one is unique

I know it will never be seen in the same way again

As it is in this precise moment

This star

This fear

This joy

This tear

Each one is unique

I know it will never be seen in the same way again

As it is in this precise moment

This child

This right

This day

This night

Each one is unique

I know it will never be seen in the same way again

As it is in this precise moment

This road

This book

This dog

This look

Each one is unique

I know it will never be seen in the same way again

As it is in this precise moment

This play

This work

This dust

This earth

Each one is unique

I know it will never be seen in the same way again

As it is in this precise moment

This friend

This breath

This life

This death

Each one is unique

I know it will never be seen in the same way again

As it is in this precise moment

This journey

This love

This beauty

This dove

Each one is unique

I know it will never be seen in the same way again

As it is in this precise moment

THE HEAVY GRUDGE NOW GONE

I don't know the reason I still carry this heavy grudge
All it does is weigh me down

I should let it fall from my shoulders

I should bury it in the ground.

I've been carrying it for so long

I can't even remember when it began

I can't even remember what it was about

Now it feels a part of me

I just can't seem to let it go

I guess I'll never be free.

Yes, I can let it go

I can!

I can and I will!

The words flowed through my mind

Let it go!

It's not doing me any good

It's making me blind to the beauty around me.

I'll write a letter to her

This woman who used to be my best friend

I'll pick up the phone and maybe we can talk

We can try to put the words behind us

The words that led to the moments of anger

The moments of anger that ruined our friendship

Maybe we can put them in the past where they belong

Why should I let this heavy grudge ruin any more of my life?

I wonder if she remembers it

It's more than time to let it go.

Today is a brand new day

Pristine and untouched

Today is the day I'll open up the door of my heart

If I can't open the door of my heart then I will open a window

Today is the day I'll get rid of this heavy grudge

I'll get rid of it once and for all

Today is the day!

I looked up her number and was amazed

She lived less than seven blocks from me!

Maybe I had passed her on the street

Maybe even talked to her before now and not realized it

My fingers were trembling as I dialed her number

She answered and recognized my voice

We began to talk as if nothing had happened

As if nothing had come between us

Soon enough the memory of that night slipped out

We talked about the heavy grudge

We looked at it every which way

We argued about it

We each admitted that we had hurt each other

We agreed to bury the heavy grudge

We buried it right there and then

We buried it right where we stood

Then we laughed

I felt better and so did she.

Later that day, I sat waiting for her in a local coffee shop

Unbidden, the question came to mind:

Why on earth had we wasted all those years?

DEAR GOD

Dear God:

Thank You for this brand new day

For my family, friends and relatives I do pray

I say a prayer for the sick

For the lonely

I say a prayer for the homeless

For the unemployed

For the elderly

I say a prayer for all those who have no one left to pray for them

I pray for peace in the world with all my heart

I say a prayer that all evil and greed will depart

I say a prayer for all the victims of war

Of terrorism

For those who are still crying

For those who are still trying to forget the horror of 9/11

I pray for all those who have died

I pray for all the souls in Purgatory

May they one day see the shining Light of Your Love.

Dear God:

Blessed Trinity – Father, Son and Holy Spirit

I thank You for guiding my footsteps this day

I thank You for showing me the way

For carrying me when I was weak

For strengthening me when trouble came knocking at my door

Now I pray that You will watch over me as I sleep

Watch over me this night

Watch over the people I love

Keep us safe from harm

Lead us all to Your everlasting Light.

PART FOUR:
NEW POEMS
BLOOD IN THE SNOW

SIMPLICITY

Simple

Uncluttered

Non-complex

That's how I like my life to be

It wasn't always so

I used to have the bad habit of making my life complicated

Much more complicated than was necessary

It was cluttered with material possessions that I didn't need

Past regrets were weighing me down

There was no reason to hang on to them

I've learned to let go of the past

Whatever has happened has happened

There's nothing at all I can do about it now

Nothing

Nothing except to learn from my mistakes

Nothing

Nothing except try not to make the same mistake twice

That's not easy to do but I try

These days I try to keep my life simple

I try to practice positive thinking

I am grateful for my blessings

I explore my senses

I embrace my present

I embolden my future by the actions I take today

I do my best to keep my life

Simple

THANKSGIVING DAY

What am I thankful for on this Thanksgiving Day?

On this Thanksgiving Day of 2008

I thank God for my health

For the love I share with my family

With my friends

For the love I share with my husband

For every smile

For every hug

For every touch

For every kiss

I thank God for the blue sky above

For the green grass below

For autumn leaves

For spring flowers

For songbirds

I am thankful for the precious memories of my life

Memories kept safe in my mind

Memories kept safe in my heart

For beautiful sights

For peaceful nights

I thank God for all the people who have touched my life

For all those who have helped me through times of trouble

Yes

There have been times of trouble for me

Times of sorrow

Times of woe

Times when my life was put on hold

A huge mountain of worry enveloped me

How would I get out of this mess?

I've lost count of the times I've asked myself that question

There have been times of illness

Times when I thought I wouldn't see the light of day again

I'm still here!

I'm here!

I'm still here!

I thank God that I'm still here!

There were times in the recent past when the whole world was in terrible turmoil

Everything was turned on its head

Everything was upside down

Everything was backwards

When big financial institutions collapsed

When jobs disappeared at an alarming rate

When people just didn't know what to do

They didn't know if they would survive the situation

There didn't seem to be any way out of it

No way around it

No way through it

The entire world was in crisis

With prayer

With hours and hours

With hours upon hours of discussion

With compromise

With prayer

Things got slowly better

At a snail's pace things got better

People breathed a sigh of relief

Thank You, God!

I thank God for my country

My country Canada

For wide open spaces

For mountains

For waterfalls

For trees

For wildlife

For flowers

For the diversity of people who live here

I thank God for my Guardian Angel

He or she guards me

He or she guides me through life's winding roads

Through detours

Through valleys

Most of all I thank God for His precious Love

For His Mercy

For the Gift of His Son

Without God where would I be?

BLOOD IN THE SNOW

I don't remember falling

One minute I'm watching my dog play in the snow

The next minute I'm flat on my face

My foot must have found some ice

I don't remember standing up

My Guardian Angel must have helped me

Blood was running down the right side of my face

It dripped onto my coat

From there it dripped to the ground

Odin and I walked back to the hotel room

I wiped the blood from my face

There was a deep cut above my right eye

My husband, Keith, called the person at reception

This kind gentleman gave us directions to the Peterborough
Hospital

Thank the Lord it wasn't far

We made it there without incident

Odin was a good dog

He stayed in the car

He could sense something was amiss.

Keith and I waited in the emergency department

The minutes ticked by

They turned into hours

One, two, three hours passed

Still we waited

Patiently we waited

Another hour slipped by

I was now growing impatient

Finally a doctor saw me

He closed the cut

Keith and I left emergency

I knew that I would be all right

Odin was glad to see us.

It was very late when we arrived back at the hotel

Keith, Odin and I were tired

We were together though

To me

That was all that mattered.

IT'S JUST YOU

It's not the words you say

It's not the things you do

It's not the love you give me

My man

My love

My husband

It's just you.

It's not the promises you keep

It's not the tears you make me weep

It's not that I know you're there for me

My man

My love

My husband

It's just you.

It's not the smile on your face

It's not that we have our own little place

It's not your arms, your warm embrace

My man

My love

My husband

My Valentine forever

It's just you.

LOVE

Love is mysterious

Love is overwhelming

Love shines in your eyes

Love shows in your smile

Love trembles in the expression on your face.

Love takes you beyond yourself

Love takes you into someone else's life

Love can make you wait forever

Until the right person comes along

You will somehow know

You will know with the first kiss

Your heart will overflow with delight

You will think of that person day and night.

Love can make your change your ways

Love will brighten up your darkest days

You don't understand

It's so strange what is happening to you

It's strange but it's wonderful too

You don't understand

Why is there magic in the air?

Why is love all around you?

Why do you feel the way you do?

In the very deepest part of you

You know that this love is for real

You know that this love is meant to be

Alas I must tell you

Love can sometimes be frustrating

Sometimes love can be complicated

Sometimes love can even be cruel

Sometimes love won't put you on cloud nine

Sometimes it will throw you in the pit instead

It will make a fool of you

Sometimes this is true

What do you do then?

Perhaps the person wasn't right for you

I was hurt in love before I found my true love

Before I found my soul mate

He was hurt too

Let your heart heal

Try again

I believe that there is someone for everyone

It took me a long time before I found my true love.

True love is a mystery

True love is overwhelming

True love changes your life forever

True love is worth the wait

True love never comes too early

It never comes too late

True love comes exactly on time.

I REMEMBER

When we walk hand in hand
When we leave footprints in the snow
When we watch the autumn leaves fall
I remember.

When I feel your gentle touch
When I feel your lips on mine
When you reach for me during the night
I remember.

When I feel your arms around me
When you chase my bad dreams away
When I lie awake and watch you sleep
I remember.

When one of your headaches comes on
When it puts you down for the day
When we have to cancel the plans we made
When I massage your head to help the pain go away
I remember.

When you go out and forget the time
When you make me worry

When I feel your love around me

I remember.

I remember why I fell in love with you

There's no one else like you

There's no one else like you in the entire world

No one else would ever do.

When we agree to disagree

When we make a difficult choice

When I know that no one loves me the way you do

I remember.

THE KIND OF DAY

It's raining outside

It's foggy

It's windy

It's the kind of day for staying indoors

The kind of day for watching television

For listening to the radio

For reading a good book

For snuggling with my husband

The kind of day to enjoy each other's company

It's the kind of day for us to be together.

It's sunny outside

There's a blue sky

It's warm

It's beautiful

It's the kind of day to be outside

For sitting on the park bench

For watching the squirrels

For listening to the songbirds

For feeding the sparrows and the starlings

For observing the parade of people as they hurry past

For my husband and I to hold hands

The kind of day for to delight in each other's company

It's the kind of day for us to be together.

MOTHER'S DAY

This is a wish to my mother

This is a wish to my sister

This is a wish to my friends

To all those who are blessed with motherhood

I hope your day is filled with smiles

I hope it is filled with unexpected surprises

I hope it is filled with special moments

Moments that will remain as precious memories

Precious memories in your heart

I hope your day is filled with love.

THE LORD OF ALL CREATION

I see the flashes of lightning

I hear the roaring thunder in the distance

I feel the cool rain on my face

And I praise the Lord of all Creation for His Glory.

I hear the buzz of the busy bee

I smell the fragrance of a flower

I see the autumn leaves floating to the ground

And I praise the Lord of all Creation for His Glory.

I hear the whispers of the breeze

I see the Canada Geese on the wing

I feel my husband's lips on mine

And I praise the Lord of all Creation for His Glory.

I see the sunlight shining on the lake

I see the full face of the moon

I feel the green grass beneath my bare feet

And I praise the Lord of all Creation for His Glory.

I feel the darkness of the night surround me

I hear the beautiful music on the radio

I feel my husband's arms around me

And I praise the Lord of all Creation for His Glory.

YOUR BIRTHDAY

Your birthday is to celebrate you

Your uniqueness

Your accomplishments

Your talents

Your courage

Your friendship

Even your disappointments

Even your frustrations

They all belong to you

No one else do they belong to

There is no one else like you in the entire world

Your single steps

Your leap of faith

Your mind

Your body

Your spirit

Your life

Your birthday is for you to celebrate yourself

So let's celebrate

Let's celebrate the day that you were born

Let's celebrate you!

REJOICE

When all the angry bitter words have been spoken
When all the fighting is through
When all the war machines have rusted in the sand
Then will we let peace rule the earth?

When all the soldiers have passed on
When a new generation of children has been born
When they begin to treat each other differently
With respect
With dignity
Then will they give peace a chance to rule the earth?

When they ask: "What are we fighting for?"
When bitter enemies slowly become friends
When they refuse to fight any more
Then the whole world will rejoice
Then peace will rule the earth.

I REMEMBER

If I do something
If I do nothing
I remember to just be

If I do something

If I do nothing

I remember to just listen

If I do something

If I do nothing

I remember to just see

If I do something

If I do nothing

I remember to just breathe

If I do something

If I do nothing

I remember to just forgive

If I do something

If I do nothing

I remember to just let go

If I do something

If I do nothing

I remember to just love

If I do something

If I do nothing

I remember to just pray

If I do something

If I do nothing

I remember to just smile

If I do something

If I do nothing

I remember to just be

CHLOE

She's a little dog

She has brown eyes

She has butterfly ears

She was born in the country

My husband and I bought her

She now lives in the big city of Toronto with us

So many changes the little dog has been through

So many changes for her new humans too

She still has a few fears

She still has a few things to learn

We are working on those together

Chloe, my husband and I

She will be okay

She will be our companion for many years to come

She is with us to stay

This little dog

The Papillon

This little Papillon named Chloe

A SPECIAL DAY

This is a brand new day in history
This has never happened before

This is history in the making

A day of change

A day of expectation

A day of hope

A day of belief

What is he thinking?

What is the first ever black African-American President thinking?

He sees the throngs of people

They are relying on him

It is a heavy burden he bears

This is a day of symbolism

A day of new thinking

A day of enthusiasm

A day of unity

A day to witness

A day to remember forever

A day of promise

This is a day like never before

Dear God

Give Obama strength

Give him courage

Give him wisdom

Give him the right people to advise him

Give him the chance to make things better

STILL LIFE

The silk flowers in the vase

The cup in the sink

The pen on the table

The book on the chair

The apple on the plate

They are all still life

Are they?

The silk flowers bring me pleasure

From the cup I drank my coffee

With the pen I wrote this poem

The book I will read some day soon

The apple I will eat